Eye of the

ALSO BY RONALD MORAN

POETRY
(books and chapbooks)

The Tree in the Mind
The Jane Poems
Waiting
The Blurring of Time
Diagramming the Clear Sky
Saying These Things
Greatest Hits, 1965-2000
Fish Out of Water
Getting the Body to Dance Again
Sudden Fictions
Life on the Rim
So Simply Means the Rain

CRITICISM

Four Poets and the Emotive Imagination (co-author)
Louis Simpson

Eye of the World

RONALD MORAN

CLEMSON
UNIVERSITY
PRESS

Works produced at Clemson University by the Center for Electronic and Digital Publishing (CEDP), including *The South Carolina Review* and its themed series "Virginia Woolf International," "Ireland in the Arts and Humanities," "James Dickey Revisited," and "African American Literature," may be found at our website: http://www.clemson.edu/cedp. Contact the director at 864-656-5399 for information.

Published by Clemson University Press at the Center for Electronic and Digital Publishing, Clemson University, Clemson, South Carolina.

Produced with the Adobe InDesign Creative Cloud and Microsoft Word. This book is set in Adobe Garamond Pro and was printed by Ricoh USA.

Editorial Assistant: Sam Martin

Webcasting and design by Charis Chapman.

Cover art by Kara McKlemurry

To order copies, contact the Center for Electronic and Digital Publishing, Strode Tower, Box 340522, Clemson University, Clemson, South Carolina 29634-0522. An order form is available on our website.

Table of Contents

❧

Acknowledgments

Grateful acknowledgment is made to the editors of the following publications in which many of these poems appeared:

Abbey: "Sonnet of the Last One" and "Sunset in Upstate South Carolina"

The Avalon Literary Review: "Illuminated" and "The Other Side of Marietta"

Big River Poetry Review: "My Father's Basement in the Night"

The Blue Hour: "A Birthday Poem," "Late Spring," and "The Rubber Room"

Boston Poetry Review: "Three Girls Playing Violin" and "View from a High Footbridge"

Chiron Review: "Bar Talk" and "Mug Shots"

Evening Street Review: "Betty Jean"

Iodine Poetry Journal: "Missing Person"

The Lake: "Attic Squirrels," "My Father's Telescope," and "The Poetry Rainbow"

The Main Street Rag: "Elevator Parties" and "Setting the Short Mark in the Long Jump"

The Orange Room Review: "The Mailbox"

Reckless Writing Poetry Anthology 2013: "Another Crossing," "I Have Commerce," and "My Father, Last Night"

Red Elf Review: "My Hungarian"

The South Carolina Review: "The Copperhead and My Mother, New Britain, 1948," "February," "Fish in a Small Tank," "Nightscapes," "The Porch in Back," and "September Again"

Stickman Review: "Still Trying"

Tar River Poetry: "The Opiate of the Sleepless"

Wild Goose Poetry Review: "Early Summer," "Eye of the World," and "Flying Over the Catskills, 1957"

for Maren O. Mitchell

Part One

EYE OF THE WORLD

Maybe all the eyes in our world may be wrong
                    (that is,
the eyes of the people) except for my right eye,
                    which
nearly eliminates the expression *too skinny*
                    from
our lexicon, since, well, it adds bulk to everything
                    it sees,

but it also adds height and, proportionately,
                    whatever
is needed to make a body or thing look natural,
                    yet larger,
and who is to say my right eye is not the eye
                    of our world,
the one eye that records dimensions as they
                    actually

are, a spin of nature revealing a truth nobody
                    will admit,
and it would not be the first time in our history,
                    that
the truth revealed itself to only one person—in
                    this case,
an older guy in South Carolina, ordinary, yet
                    possessed

with a certain eye power that makes most people
                    look better,
physically larger, more in command, which is what
                    most want,
and who spend huge amounts of money for eyes
                    and surgeons,
when what they really want are what they have
                    always.

My Father's Telescope

took both of us to set it up on our front porch,
and whenever we did, I could never focus it,

just as I could not focus on much then, at nine,
my mind too soft, too spongy to grasp figures

in the sky, the constellations my father called
out to me on our walks on Leon Street, after

supper in the colder months, saying, *Look!
There's Taurus the Bull,* and so I stayed silent

as a prop, while his body and mind locked
into a universe alive for him. Later, under

streetlights in Philadelphia and New Britain,
anywhere, my shadow began to lengthen;

one night I caught up with it and never let it go.
Above, the heavens kept shining for my father.

THE COPPERHEAD AND MY MOTHER, NEW BRITAIN, 1948

Snakes lounged on the wall in our back yard
                    as soon
as my father built it—two feet high, where
                    our
our property started sloping toward a creek,
                    in a small
gap between fields of weeds and scrub oaks.
                    To him,

stone walls were no home to snakes. Wrong.
                    Together,
king snakes, blacksnakes and copperheads
                    sunned
in peace, side by side, on the warm stones
                    of his
great wall. And me at twelve—I kept my
                    distance,

letting the snakes follow whatever course
                    they chose.
Whatever aroused their interest, OK by me.
                    One
late June afternoon, my mother, tending
                    her
flowers, saw a copperhead on the top level
                    of our

backyard, retrieved her hoe, tried to kill it,
                    slipping
and falling, her head landing only four inches
                    directly
in front of the copperhead, who, as it turned
                    out,
displayed perfect manners and slithered back
                    home.

SETTING THE SHORT MARK IN THE LONG JUMP

While I was not flying, I did stay in the air
                    as if
I were floating, but no more than two feet
                    above
ground before I touched down, making me
                    feel
as good as I could in a dream, my drifting
                    slightly
above the intractable earth, and, if no one
                    saw me,
I knew I had done it; and, on waking up,
                    I was
exhilarated, believing I was the first to float
                    on air.
Then, I thought, *Why did I dream about this?*
                    After

discounting all my wine and sugary yogurt,
                    I recalled
how, as a long jumper in my freshman year
                    at college,
I disappointed everyone—the track coach
                    who never
knew my name, my teammates when my
                    turn came,
and me trying to force my reluctant body
                    to take off,
so coach and my teammates would say,
                    in awe,
We never thought Ron could ever do that!
                    which
I did only once, without trying, while sound
                    asleep.

MY HUNGARIAN

My mother was Hungarian, and she would
never let me remember it, by Anglicizing
her maiden name, by forbidding me from
telling anyone that I was half Hungarian,
refusing to teach me any Magyar, despite
my asking during childhood and the teens.
I could never speak with my grandparents,
who were not taught how to speak English.

When I was just 16, I dated a Polish girl, warm,
sweet. I liked her, and I think she felt the same
about me, but when my mother found out
she was of Slavic descent, she shut the door.
I want to apologize to her for my absence
of courage over 60 years ago, howsoever late.

THE OPIATE OF THE SLEEPLESS

I am trying to drift off in my bed after two
        taxing
weeks while the medical profession puzzled
        over
what might be clogging my arteries, since
        I scored

off the books in some arcane calcium test
        and since
my left leg blew up from the knee down,
        as if
pumped with air, but tests were negative;
        and now

I want only to let myself fall asleep, taking
        whatever
time I can get, with radio as the opiate
        of my mass—
my sleeping aid, my tranquilizer—but not
        tonight,

when, on the first talk show I dial in, I hear
        a caller
saying he is barefoot, with his gun resting
        in his lap,
while the host, hearing such welcome news,
        applauds him

for exercising his Second Amendment rights,
        both
agreeing that tea parties are the only hope
        left for us;
so I try again, this time finding a talk show
        with two guys

calling each other *Doctor* every 90 seconds,
        plus
spending over half their time between ads
        knocking
our drug industry, as if it accounts for all
        elderly

traumas in America. I think they must be
                    chiropractors
or out-of-round nutritionists. I turn it off,
                    get up,
go into my kitchen, pour myself a drink,
                    then another.

I HAVE COMMERCE

with the dead and dying as they were at
the height of their living. In my dreams,
they command and I comply too easily, as
if their presence completes my emptiness,

my so quick willingness to agree. *Yes, Yes,*
I do understand. Which way to the crest?
I leaned too far, without thinking or cause,
over the edge of a roof of a tall building,

listening to death's syntax, its raw tongues;
and with my fingers like claws, I gripped
the indifferent stone. *I'm not ready yet.*
The dead and dying took up sides over me:

they cheered me on and wept, they offered
advise and consent in a burnished blue sky.
I could neither hold on nor let the edge deny
me, but they kept at it. *Let go. No, Hold on.*

The Porch in Back

I'm finally sitting in one of the two chairs
                    on
the porch I had built on my deck five years
                    ago,
the porch being Ron's folly; but at one time
                    I thought,

well, this is a good place to entertain, if I
                    entertained,
which I didn't but talked myself into it,
                    thinking,
why not turn it into a porch I could enjoy,
                    sitting here

with a woman, she sipping a Vodka Collins,
                    with a dash
of orange, while for me, Jim Beam on the rocks,
                    both of us
listening to the easy tones of wind chimes,
                    the occasional

bark of a small dog, breed unknown, while
                    we watch
late afternoon change its clothes for evening,
                    as we continue
sipping, talking, watching, as if we were here
                    together.

NIGHTSCAPES

I am sitting in my den, my head hissing
like a leak in a forced air line, but nothing
ever comes out, not even something as
small as the letter *i* or a cone of air rising
from an iron, hissing except when I sleep;
but every night since Jane left, my dreams

are bizarre, out of round, like being lost
in a strange building, no time left to fix
my being late, always lost and late—
so last night, after my wine, I pleaded
with Jane to return in my sleep, to calm
my night life, so that, when I woke up

the next morning, my body would cease
its usual dance. Last night, I slept without
dreaming, woke calm as if I were a child,
and thanked her, as I have since her death,
for changing my life, this time for coming
back to do the same, for the better, again.

Spinning Out of Round

I am in my bedroom and the room is spinning
                    rapidly,
so I am trying to figure out why, when the phone
                    rings.
Without looking at its screen, I pick it up, not
                    even
sure if the phone really did ring or whether it
                    was

an auditory hallucination, given circumstances
                    of the room's
revolutions until, finally, I lie down on my back,
                    close my eyes,
hoping to disarm the spinning mechanism, while
                    I say,
Hello. This is Ron, to the dial tone, when I realize
                    the room

is still, and I am so pleased with my miraculous
                    recovery,
I begin a conversation with the dial tone, which
                    is
one-sided, so I say to myself, *I need a drink,*
                    get
out of bed, go to the refrigerator for a cold beer
                    or wine.

Finding nothing there but milk, juice, a lemon,
                    and
assorted non-mind-altering items, I return
                    to bed,
waiting for something in my room to levitate,
                    or to see
a sign in the dark, withheld from me all my life,
                    taking shape.

ANOTHER CROSSING

I raise my eyebrows twice, as if I were a signalman
                          on deck
receiving messages, when someone asks, *Are you
                          living*
in sin? I reply, *If by **sin** you mean not sanctioned
                          by law—*
whose law? While not arrogant, I am playful, since
                          if I were
to be condemned to an afterlife of being denied
                          passage

across the river—the boatman not yet convinced
                          to let me
cross, to begin another life, maybe even redeem
                          myself
if I am worthy—I should try to make the best of it.
                          Shouldn't I?
So, Love, whoever you are, come along, wait until
                          the goddess
tells the boatman to take us on, to deliver us both
                          to the marsh.

SPS

It is time now for the obligatory closure,
        as if
I were patronized by the exotic dancer
        of my
conscience, the one that gyrates around
        a pole,

her tight breasts on fire, tipped with lust.
        Why
has it become so important I take a stand
        now,
when all I really want to do is pass these
        frayed

years in friendship, not lust or back room
        antics?
I want to free myself from a band of steel
        tightly
wrapped around my head, when all I hear
        is my

dead father saying, *SPS*, to all complaints—
        Self Pity Stinks—
while I try to figure out how to accept what
        I am,
and I remember my pastor's sermon today,
        Forgiveness,

so I ask myself, Maybe I am not enough
        by myself?
What sacramental pardon is suitable or
        needed?
Is confession insufficient, too broad to be
        acceptable?

STILL TRYING

I am, as one might expect, in my den still trying
                    to gauge
the parameters of my universe, failing, as usual,
                    in the best
way I can, since, well, the blinds of my windows
                    are
closing more rapidly than before, even though
                    I want

to know, despite my having been instructed,
                    in no
uncertain terms, to cease my forever queries,
                    to work
at accepting the inevitable, to ease off, enjoy,
                    even
relish those rare moments of earned delight
                    while

I strain, trying to measure chunks of skylight
                    nearly,
 but not completely, hidden by the rapacious
                    limbs
of an oak tree I thought wrongly responsible
                    for my
once hearty Bermuda dying in its shade, only
                    to learn

I was the agent of its death, another instance
                    of my
still knowing I am able to learn, regardless
                    of the
the boundaries of my irrational thoughts,
                    my often
rational behavior, the long links of sorrow
                    binding them.

The Rubber Room

In the hard rubber room of limitations,
I felt my world of poetry spinning out
of orbit, like an errant satellite, burning
to ashes when it entered the atmosphere
of new cultures in our diverse paradigm—
teaching me that one must anticipate
rules will change in how poets ascend
to elite status, their names like the music
of spheres; that is, if one hopes to enter
that circle of poets whose presence rings
clear beyond subject, texture, or thought:
Star light, star bright, first star I see tonight.

My Father's Basement in the Night

My father says, *Why not show your friends my basement?*
Although I have never been there, I think it is large, old.

I reply, *Why should I?* He does not answer me. I think
he is lonely, and this time he is shorter than I remember.

My mother wanders in this house I do not remember.
I think she is sick but I do not know, yet I am worried

she may try to go outside, so I call out twice, *Mother,
where are you?* She answers, *In here,* and from a hallway

I see her legs stretched out on a bed in a room I cannot
enter, while my father is in the basement, waiting for us.

MY FATHER, LAST NIGHT

Last night, my father dropped about an inch
in height; and when we met in a cold room
I was never in before, he told me he was now
the president of a company. He was standing
in front of a tall desk, shuffling papers without

looking at them, and he had a neat mustache,
white with dark shades, which surprised me
since he never grew one before, though like
all men at one time, he tried, so when I asked
him, *Dad when did you grow that?* He said,

Yesterday and today, and I was both envious
and surprised—how he manipulated such
dimensions—and while I was trying to think
what I could do to impress him, he picked
up his briefcase and vanished through a door.

Part Two

The Other Side of Marietta

is where Auggie said he came from,
but I only knew he would show up
in a pickup that sounded like a tank,
with a different business card, new
phone number, when least expected,
saying, *Hey Ron. What can I do for you?*

That meant any kind of work any other
landscape service would not do, like
cleaning out the ravenous undergrowth
behind my slim stone wall to the creek
in back, a flood zone earning its name
at every intense downpour, even after

the county cleaned out the creek bed,
drained the toxic pond where the creek
emptied, leaving the area behind my wall
still venomous, with only Auggie willing
to risk going in there; and on his last visit,
he said, *Hey Ron. Guess what? I got one.*

Got one what? What're you talking about?
I said, in response to his wide, contagious
smile, one that stretched across his face,
his teeth white as ivory—*A copperhead,
Ron, and I killed it, so you don't have to
after he gets you, my good friend.* I said,
Thanks Auggie. Be careful in that tank.

BAR TALK

I'm sitting on a stool at my local bar,
where this guy I never saw before is
currying favor with the cute bartender.
Since I'm the only other person there,
I try to say something to him while
he stirs his drink. He responds, as if
he were in court, answering a hostile
question repeated by a prosecutor.

Where do I go from here? Should I tell
him I was only hoping to make contact
with another human, or should I sit back,
stir the memory of my wine-bruised mind,
then wait for some sign saying, *You're OK?*

Mug Shots

In our visual ascendancy, the alleged murderers,
rapists, child molesters, terrorists, kidnappers
are all pictured alike, with faces drawn, lips tight,
turned downward, hair unruly, giving an impression
that, hey, you would not want your daughter, son,
sister, brother, or friend you loved, or even one
cared about, to hook up with, and I want to know
why these depictions are always menacing, even
before an indictment or conviction? Why not
(*aka* an alleged suspect) look at ease, like pictures
of your family in the living room or in a hallway space,
if not smiling, not so unsavory you'd want to cross
any street before having to meet one face to face?

VIEW FROM A HIGH FOOTBRIDGE

At dusk, I watch the first-love couples walk
                    a trail
above this rocky but free-flowing river,
                    its
banks steeped in arrogance, its currents
                    bizarre.

The luckier ones know that love, like a laser,
                    cuts
through the soft veneer of innocence, thus
                    revealing
shock and delight that enlighten and clarify,
                    like the clear,

cold waters of this river, unnamed, unknown;
                    but
to them, now, for the first, unforgettable time,
                    and, yes,
they want to be alone together, as all of us
                    do

or did at one time, the best time of our lives,
                    holding
and holding on until the unearthly bell began
                    tolling,
It's time, it's time enough. Find yourselves,
                    sweet loves.

BETTY JEAN

I am looking for the Betty Jean I have not seen
                    in 60 years,
who went with me to Mrs. Linder's dance recitals
                    for two years

and whose family moved back to Memphis after
                    her father died,
far too young. Before they left, I wrote to her
                    in my clumsy

and stiff early teen style, and she responded
                    gracefully,
Thank you for caring, and that was it; and now
                    I want

to know what happened to this good-hearted
                    girl who made
my two dance recitals bearable, my hair slicked
                    down

with Suave, dried to a nearly rock hardness, while
                    Betty Jean
never chided me for my missteps or self-conscious
                    indifference.

My friend, my first partner, where are you?
                    I want
to talk with you, tell you how sorry I am for what
                    I did not do.

THE SEASON OF FLESH

In the season of flesh, short shorts climb
                              another
inch over last year, taut and tanning
                              skins slope
toward bejeweled navels, waist lines
                              narrow,
true to fashions, and no one would ever
                              object
to the arc of thighs capturing the dream
                              of
every guy, and now, I guess, some girls,
                              too—
this flesh in late-May abundance where
                              I live
in Upstate SC, air crisp, flesh unlocking
                              more
portals: legs, backs, necks, feet, wherever
                              flesh,
proverbial crawler, finds willing openings
                              to enter.

Legacy of the Zany

I believe I get the draw of Language Poetry
in the last half of the Twentieth Century,
when I was neither in the mainstream nor,
indeed, in any *au courant* rivulet, while
poets and movements were thriving or dying
on the precious whims of editors, and choices
of lines, subjects, ideas, stanzas, spacing, even
punctuation, if used, abused, or even excused.

Now, when I read a poem in an elite journal
and I do not recognize the name of the poet,
I am ready for that poem to invite me into it,
so that I might find the legacy of poetry some
forty years ago, probably not as bizarre now,
more coherent, shaped, but still zany, I hope.

THE FLIP SIDE OF JOY

I'm thinking of joy, an abstraction or woman—
                    though
 I don't know anyone named Joy but I think
                    I must have
elsewhere, in a different time, when names
                    of women
favored abstractions, though mostly biblical—
                    while

I'm reading a novel by Richard Russo where,
                    after
fifty pages, he names the heroine Joy, though
                    there's
slight kinship between her name and character.
                    Outside
the temperature is in the upper 90s; the birds
                    that began

bickering at daybreak take hot siestas or else
                    guard
against the moist hungers of timber rattlers,
                    copperheads;
and I wonder, as a child, how my sweet Polly,
                    a collie
with a mighty nose, found a circuitous path
                    around

all snakes to the hill bottom, on mornings when
                    my father
had to drag out of bed, open the back door, let
                    her out,
wait for her to return, then go back to sleep,
                    a troubled sleep
for all of us then, as Joy, the angel of our dreams,
                    slept through us.

ILLUMINATED

Yes, to be illuminated
        and not

by any particular source,
        but say,

the fragrant shimmers
        of her

passing by, as she tosses
        lightly

off the lightness of gifts,
        corridors,

of enviable rooms opened
        but once.

FISH IN A SMALL TANK

I was sitting in my den, a small fish in a tank,
                    when
I thought of the word *notable* in a context
                    I do not
remember, if ever there were any context,
                    given

the broad sweep of lethargy that became
                    my caregiver;
but the word would not let me loose, so
                    I let it
guide me, as if it mapped an escape route
                    for a small

captive fish, if the fish felt it was captive,
                    all of which
led me to the fundamental paradox
                    of both
notable and *not able,* including that fish
                    still swimming

circles in the clear barrier glass of its life
                    through
which, maybe, it saw a means of escape,
                    along
with the means of its absolute drowning
                    in air.

GERM OF SPIRIT

Early in a novel, I came across the phrase
          germ of spirit,
which first attracted, then puzzled me,
                    given
its context—used to describe a six year
              old boy

of unknown parentage whose mind was
              as clear
as his deep-set gray eyes. By my trying
              to yoke
germ to *spirit,* I uncovered what I never
              could

earlier—a natural compatibility of the two,
              foretelling
what would happen to this stunning child,
                who
then gained the power to alter what others
              thought

to be their destinies; and, well, what do any
              of us
ever know, but by reaching as far as we can
                with
whatever texts lie before us, and, then, even
              further?

ELEVATOR PARTIES

During 1969-70, in Würzburg, West Germany,
the guest workers from Greece and Turkey who
maintained our tall apartment building also lived
on two of its lower floors, and by Friday noon
they were well into celebrating the weekend,
juiced and joyous in our only elevator, hopping
from one leg to the other, dancing jigs, while
thick, long-bodied eels—their delicacy caught
in the Main River—dangled over their arms,
and they rocked so long and hard in our elevator
it finally gave out; so residents who lived higher
climbed, our weekly exercise, to the acrid smell
of eels cooking, our company on the long climb.

The Poetry Rainbow

I

At the end of the poetry rainbow, instead
of finding
the golden tablet of words, one may learn
that any
extant poem is still subject to an unnerving
scrupulosity,
and thus be wary of offering a new poem,
for fear
it was written before, then having to listen
to a soft voice
echoing in a huge, nearly noiseless chamber,
Guilty.

II

No, poetry is never the right button to push
for
scientists who delight in deconstructing
emotive
responses, as if lines of poetry were suspect,
since love
cannot be quantified, even by its apologists
or its
antagonists, when all of us look for the same
reward
at the end, all we want to be able to say is,
Yes. O Yes.

Part Three

Flying Over the Catskills

Nearly 50 years ago I was flying southeast
out of Buffalo, on a French jet whose name
I cannot remember, where I sat up front
on a flight so smooth and quiet I felt
I entered a dreamscape, looking out
over the Catskills in January, white
as rapture, trees like fingers beckoning.

So taken was I with this enticement
from a world that was discovering me,
I thought, Should I answer it now
or cling forever to this calling out to me?
But I failed to act, holding within myself,
too distant and deep, what held me then.

FEBRUARY

I

February, last month for celebrations, except
                    funerals,
the steep climb of deaths during winter's peak,
                    not
only because of its being trimmed back short,
                    but also,
February sits between winter and spring, like
                    a child
at the most awkward age, all skinny legs, arms,
                    no shape
or form upon which to guess what will follow:
                    if muscles
will firm up strong, if legs and arms will stretch,
                    body inhaling
deeply the elixir of growing life—all the while
                    February
hesitating, between asserting itself as the first
                    sign
of spring and then retracting all, when snow like
                    a shroud
covers the budding grounds in the upstate fields
                    of South Carolina;
and I am thinking of a gawky, not yet bulked up
                    boy
in middle school—how unfair to be bully bait,
                    like
some of the elderly must feel in their final rooms
                    on earth.

II

I say, *Hey, February, I need you, as all of us do,*
                    to shake
our bodies free from excess waters, seasonally
                    before March,
the month of decisions for us, whether we are
                    bound
by the cold or free to explore the delicate greens
                    of life.

LATE SPRING

I am trying to figure out why I am committed
          to
this flood zone in back where nothing gives
          up its
iron-like grip on our lack of immunity from
          the death

of small birds, carriers of the West Nile virus,
          or from
the season's growing impatience, like heavy
          rains
while the nervous cars in my neighborhood
          run

every stop sign; and a half dozen houses up
          my street,
a boy of four plays at the end of his driveway,
          darting
across the street to capture an errant ball.
          I pray

he will live long enough to know his folly,
          since, well,
his parents appear not to; and yesterday
          when
I drove into my neighborhood, I saw a car
          eager

to ignore a stop sign, its driver bent over her
          cell phone,
the car obeying her orders; when she saw
          me,
she slammed on the brakes, her Chevy's rear
          raising

like the head of a cobra, and I starting thinking
          of all
the pythons in the Everglades, having already
          eliminated
the population of squirrels, rabbits, and small
          deer.

And, hey, with the globe warming, when will
                                        they discover
South Carolina, will I live that long, and if I do,
                                        will I step
out into the near dark, hearing nothing there
                                        and be taken?

On a Summer Night, 1957

It is never the same, is it? The moment when
                    you fall
in love, the instant when you know nothing else
                    matters,
only how you feel about her, whether or not
                    she

reciprocates. Perhaps she will, if not now, then
                    maybe
in the fixed future, and if she does you will have
                    the moment
stored in your memory box, though you will
                    notice

others, perhaps—even think they are interested
                    in you;
but that first moment will never disappear while
                    locked
in your mind. I remember my first date with Jane
                    in 1957:

it was on a summer night when her brother, Dick
                    (my best friend),
and Roger, another friend of ours, and I were just
                    hanging
around the rec room of Dick and Jane's house—
                    Jane and I

knowing each other for nine years but never dating—
                    but that day
her cousin and a friend were spending an overnight
                    with Jane,
so, with all of us in the rec room, all six unconnected,
                    Dick said,

Let's hit the road, go somewhere fun. We did,
                    to The Cabin,
a teenage roadhouse in Cromwell, Connecticut.
                    That night,
I asked Jane to dance with me to the song *Tammy*,
                    during which

I fell in love with her, that quickly. And I never
stopped,
even though we had to conquer some obstacles,
and we did,
lived as man and wife for 50 years, until death
did us part.

EARLY SUMMER

My friend writes that he hopes *I am staying cool*
                    during
the worst heat spell in the recorded history of
                    South Carolina,
known for, among other things, its hot, muggy
                    summers,

the air thick enough to take away the breath
                    of our
elderly and very young in July and August, but
                    not on
our beaches or high up in the Blue Ridge Range;
                    and while

I may not be staying as cool as I want, I am cool
                    enough
and thankful I do not have to worry about floods,
                    grassfires,
blizzards, ice storms, tornadoes, and earthquakes
                    here,

in my corner of our state, between mountains
                    and flatlands,
the Piedmont, where I admit to the possibility
                    of nature
exercising its bad temper but I will not admit to
                    its probability.

Sunset in Upstate South Carolina

It is a late June evening, the sky is somber,
        a light
rain is falling, nothing is moving except
        leaves
stirred slightly by sparse drops of rain,
        and air

is a pale yellow, not from pollen, as usual,
        but
from the sun signing off behind low clouds,
        and I start
to think of a walkway I used many years
        ago,

three tall stories up, joining two buildings,
        where
once I saw a stunning sunset over a lake,
        a brilliant
montage of sun, sky, and cloud—ecstatic,
        like rapture,

unlike now, when I must not dwell on then,
        instead
focus on the silence of the scene before me,
        its
message tentative, indefinite, and baffling,
        like love fading.

SEPTEMBER AGAIN

One more day in September when I have not yet
                    contracted
the going virus, whatever it is, since public schools
                    are back
doing contagion rituals, just as vacationers return
                    from exotic places
with long-lived bacteria in travel bags and edgy
                    colons,

while Congress is more queasy in September than
                    usual,
when called back early into session, no matter
                    whatever
menace is on the table: saran gas used in Syria,
                    nuclear
threats from underdeveloped countries like Iran,
                    but, how

underdeveloped? since they think they are ready
                    to prove
their potency, while the UN balks at sending teams,
                    and who
can blame them, what with all the key stockpiles
                    of evidence
off limits, like cheerleaders to acne-faced boys
                    in high school.

Off limits, sure, the sad projections of countries
                    on the edge,
just as these boys, together in groups in the halls,
                    make up
a country without a flag, but who may someday
                    enjoy chic condos
on the stark Maine coastline, above virulent tidal
                    waters.

ATTIC SQUIRRELS

Today, another one died in the closed
                    off area
of my attic, in a space like a bubble,
                    heavier
than air but still lighter than water.
                    Last year
a squirrel dug under a partition to die
                    there,

in a peace to be found nowhere else;
                    but still,
I want to know why, when it first
                    entered
my house, it acted like it's party time—
                    tap dancing,
bumping into the air ducts as if drunk,
                    maybe

on the heavy air—then, when all went
                    quiet
the piranhas of the insect world began
                    living
off of the newly dead, leaving behind
                    the pungent
smell of a carcass stiffening, it having
                    been purged.

What sounded like a raucous party might
                    have been
the hoarding of enough acorns secretly,
                    a treat
to nibble on before its long sleep settled
                    in.
So I am thinking that my guest today
                    is old:

one who knew its days in the huge nest
                    in the V
of an ancient maple out back were over,
                    my house
the nearest setting for a burial plot,
                    a space
with soft insulation to cushion a body
                    worn out.

SHARKS, JUNE 2015

In this accusatory year, one cannot fix
                    the blame
easily for shark attacks on our East coast,
                    youths
dismembered, the targets more incidental
                    than true;
and, though it's feeding season for sharks,
                    this is
the first time our coast was traumatized
                    since Jaws.
Then, as now, sharks were not after our
                    bony flesh;

and as soon as they realize their error,
                    sharks
back off, leaving us dead or maimed,
                    as if
the world of nature we support turns
                    on us,

unintentionally, but an accident too real
                    to forgive
or forget, these times when our country,
                    our world,
seems out of tune with the music we loved
                    for centuries.

Part Four

MISSING PERSON

In this age of instacom, if you're missing,
                    you're
presumed dead, gender and age aside,
                    yet if
your family thinks you lived well but still
                    outlived

your worth, all of them, near and distant,
                    will have
alibis, armored like a personnel carrier.
                    These innocents—
plus neighbors, close friends, the church
                    choir—

play their given cards in a not-so-innocent
                    questioning
by the law, since a very high percentage
                    of murders
are by someone well-known to the victim;
                    but if,

and when, the person is found unharmed,
                    maybe
waiting in a bus terminal, bench sitting
                    in City Park,
weeding flower beds in a stranger's garden,
                    unaware

of the crisis created, seemingly to have fallen
                    off one
of the four corners of Earth, they all celebrate,
                    momentarily,
the life of the one returned from certain death,
                    then mourn.

Three Girls Playing Violin

I know there are sadder things on a Sunday
                    than
listening to three pre-teen girls playing violin
                    at
the 11:00 service, but not for me that day,
                    perhaps

because both my dead parents played violin:
                    my father
at a more skilled level than the girls Sunday,
                    but my mother
would have fit right in with them, serious
                    and sincere,

as all violinists are, but their playing could
                    break
your heart, knowing how much effort these
                    three
girls put out, thin, like their bows, practicing
                    for weeks,

now playing before an audience that, out
                    of mercy,
did not drop their heads but did not applaud
                    when
it was over, looking solemn, as if they were
                    lined

up just before visitation, next to shake hands,
                    to offer
consolation to the bereaved while feeling loss,
                    yet not
needing to be strong or able to reach or touch
                    their core.

American Sad

Still trying to figure out why churchgoers
                in America
are declining in numbers, so I suggest
                cable

TV networks and sports channels may be,
                in part,
responsible, since the first and fastest
                in America

try to compel us to accede to their lure,
                the promise
of home delivery of a new, radiant life.
                Back

when church was the known, universal
                equalizer,
those controlled by spouses or bosses
                on

any ordinary work week were freed up
                by a church
in mid-week opening up its committee
                rooms

to members, thus acknowledging that,
                yes,
their voices were important, which also
                sustained

them until Sundays, when, in their pews,
                they
would sit content, at last proud of their
                standing.

THE MAILBOX

It is late Saturday afternoon and again no mail for me.
                    I think
I may be the lab rat for the end of mail deliveries
                    on Saturdays,
the one chosen by chance before the official date.
                    If so,
am I then being monitored, along with my mailbox,
                    and

is what I say or do being logged, maybe by a small
                    drone,
innocent to the untrained eye, sans missiles or bombs,
                    with only
a four-foot wingspan, like a model airplane, garage or
                    basement-born,
incapable of harm, not concealing a high-tech camera
                    or recorder?

Will my mailbox and I really be what history will record
                    as having
been the test site for the hope of the USPS, its policies
                    and future?
If so, I say here and now, this time only, while I love
                    my country,
I also love my mail and the singular feeling of opening
                    my mailbox.

THE OBITUARIES

I am losing patience with my local newspaper
for printing the same obituaries three, four
or even more days in a row, not to correct
errors, but to satisfy mourners who demand
that all in the upstate know deeply of their loss.

Some might argue, *Well, so what, who cares*
so long as they pay for it? I care, having dealt
with death too often, having been sensitized
to excesses and/or repetitions; and when I see
multiple entries of sorrow, I think about the dead.

I mean, would they want their lives and deaths
on display daily, as if on a billboard? I doubt
that is an item in their wills, not in our upstate,
where our neighbors, friends, the church, even
our long counties, already know, care, respond.

A WAR WITHOUT PITY ON THE HOME FRONT

I tried to enlist but they would not take me,
                    because
my Jane was pregnant, or I am not sure why,
                    but
I was never an object of anger in the 1960's,
                    when
the guys who went to Vietnam and returned
                    were
labeled killers or else outcasts, pariahs, after
                    going
halfway across the world, not by choice,
                    but
because our government said, *Go, kill,* but
                    never said,

Go, kill, survive, and then we will love you all.
                    My friends
who made it back still will not speak of what
                    happened
in Southeast Asia, even though now we know
                    better,
honoring them 40 years later—their dreams,
                    memories,
they kept to themselves, as if in dense foliage,
                    the Viet Cong
easily manipulated their home terrain, while
                    still waiting
on the perimeters for the openings that only
                    they knew of.

An American Version of Health

I just finished reading an issue of *On Health,*
                    a *CR*
supplement, also *AARP Magazine,* and at 78,
                    I think

I should quiver, since what I eat and drink
                    are all wrong:
and so, I wonder, how I ever made it this far,
                    and is there

time to correct my dietary and other deficits
                    before
one of the big four diseases of the elderly takes
                    me down

and/or out? Much to think about, Eh? What,
                    if anything,
to do in the fourth quarter? Suppose I make
                    a sea change

like the experts say? What about life as a sloth
                    and my
faith in processed foods since my beloved Jane
                    died

over five years ago? Maybe, I am doomed, just
                    as John Kerry
and Al Gore before him said our country is, given
                    our

neglect of *climate change* and *global warming,*
                    and I am like
a generator in a siege of rough weather, running
                    on fumes.

SMILES—*AARP THE MAGAZINE*

If not on each page, close, as if over 50 is a charm:
                    celebs
posing for ads, but not for scooters or hearing aids;
                    a couple,

in their 50s or 60s, where she exclaims, smiling,
                    TV Ears
saved our marriage! What would have happened
                    without TV Ears?

Would she have left to find a man with TV Ears?
                    Or, well,
Why didn't she just leave, with the kids grown up,
                    now

on their own, and what kind of a marriage was it,
                    if TV Ears
saved it? Or the woman, same age as cited above,
                    driving

a Hoverground she said gave her life back, but now
                    her
granddaughter can't keep up with her, the latter,
                    on roller blades,

fully equipped, with helmet, pads, a smile like
                    Grandma's.
Elsewhere, in ads or articles, always the smiles,
                    including

Dolly Parton in two large photos displaying her
                    attributes,
while making older seem younger or even better
                    for all.

Sonnet of the Last One

The one solitary person left on earth—
well, here I am, not unhappy but lonely
at times, although I have come to court
whatever is left growing as well as
anything still breathing water, air, if only
for only a finite, given, and limited time.

I promise to learn the language of hardy
forms, as well as the halting murmurs
of creatures in the sea, fast fading but what
I learn from them is astonishing and could
be life-giving, but for the near future, I am
honored to be picked, howsoever, and, yes,

I will plant all the seeds I can harbor in this
semi-fertile soil, and then I will plant myself.

SELF-DIALOGUE, THE LAST ACT

I'm trying to think of why it's so easy in my
older years to say, *Oh, it was much better
to write back then, with at least a soft buzz,*
which, when younger, seemed a cop-out.
I could never excuse my own weaknesses.

In the middle of late nights last year, my
dead Jane and father sat up in my bed.
I said, *You're fading from me again. Where
are you going?* In my weak night lite, they
were in soft colors, pastels against shadows.

With its tiring demands and vast energy, age
replied, *Get another drink. Try being at ease,*
to which I said, *OK, my friend. What do I do
after that?* No response. I lay back on my bed,
trying to wait, as usual, for what to think next.

A Note on the Poet

R onald Moran was born in Philadelphia and moved to New Britain, Connecticut, when he was 10. He received his BA from Colby College and his MA and PhD from Louisiana State University. After having taught at the University of North Carolina for nine years, he joined the Clemson University faculty in 1975, and retired twice, first in 1998 and then in 2000. He served in a number of positions at Clemson, including Professor and Head of the Department of English, Associate Dean, and Interim Dean. In 1969-70, he was Fulbright Lecturer at the University of Würzburg in Germany. He has published twelve books/chapbooks of poetry, including *Saying These Things*, the inaugural volume of poetry issued by the Clemson University Digital Press in 2004. Moran is the author of one book of literary criticism and co-author of another. His poems and essays are widely published in magazines such as *Commonweal, Emrys Journal, Evening Street Review, The Louisiana Review, Mankato Poetry Review, North American Review, Northeast, Northwest Review, South Carolina Review, Southern Review, Tar River Poetry*, and *Yankee*. Moran lives in Simpsonville, South Carolina. His work is archived in the James B. Duke Library at Furman University, and he has won numerous awards for his poetry.